I0419458

Living on the Edge of Civilization

By James Nugent

The setting

Olympia is the capital city of the State of Washington. It is the modern epicenter of politics and has a year round population of perhaps 49,000 people. When the legislature is in session the numbers grows a bit, but it remains picturesque and quiet. The Capitol dome dominates the hill on which the government building sit and the Governor's mansion overlooks the large manmade lake just to the west of the public buildings.

The seat of state government is situated at the southern terminus of Puget Sound. The 5-mile long inlet is called Budd Inlet. The polluted waters and beaches of Budd inlet are home to the Port of Olympia. The port has been a center for commercial activity for more than a century. The port has never met its potential because Tacoma is 30 miles to the north, and Seattle is 60 miles the North. They are closer for visiting ships. Although, the occasional foreign ship arrives empty and leaves with a load of logs; the port is usually quiet.

The logs which are extremely valuable are harvested from the Olympic Peninsula which is a few miles to the west of Olympia. The Olympic Peninsula is breathtakingly beautiful and full of natural wonders. A hundred years ago the Olympic Peninsula was the source of unimaginable wealth for those who owned companies that logged trees. Soon the trees were depleted. The logging companies either went out of business or moved to business model that provided for a sustainable crop of trees on a 30-year cycle, of replantation and harvesting. A satellite picture of the 3600 square mile peninsula shows the devastation of this massive natural wonder. Less than half the land is preserved as National Park. The rest of the natural ecosystem is "managed" by The National Forest Service and the trees are sold to the remaining logging companies.

Just five miles to the west of Olympia is Mud Bay. It is the terminus of Eld Inlet. This inlet has been the site of commercial shellfish harvesting for over a century. The water is clean and shellfish from this and other inlets feed most of the oyster and clam consumption for the nation.

There are bears, and cougars and bald eagles living in this area and salmon return every fall to spawn. The area has few people and the shorelines have mostly been preserved from any further development by a private consortium.

This is one of my favorite places to take a kayak and it is mentioned in several of my short stories about kayaking available at Amazon.com. I lived half way up the inlet in Young Cove for 17 years on the beach.

A mile from Mud bay there is a "y" in the road. To the right Highway 101 begins a 326-mile loop. The loop goes some 326 miles around the circumference of the Olympic Peninsula and eventually returns to Mud Bay via the pacific coast and stretch of Highway 8.

To the left Highway 8 travels to the west and what the federal government has called, "The New Appalachia." The area is from just west of Olympia out to the coast for a hundred miles of the loop. It also includes more of southwest Washington State. There is no official sign or line delineating "The New Appalachia." However, when you leave mud bay there is a different natural environment and human culture.

For a couple of years, I traveled 100 miles a day round trip to a dark little town on the coast for work. The first time I got out of the car I noticed that street lights were on even during the day nine months a year. Being located right on the Pacific Ocean the wind was strong and the rain blew sideways most of the winter. Flooding was frequent and in the Spring when the weather moderated a little, the bugs and particularly mosquitoes filled the air. I rarely got in the car without bringing a few bugs with me.

Every evening I made the 50 mile return trip. I noticed that after I was through the Black Hills and on the downhill side going to Mud Bay; the rain and fog would often clear and would be greeted with clear skies and sunshine.

But this story is not about weather. It is about living and working right on the edge of civilization, and why I eventually moved back into the city (the Olympia area).

In the beginning, I lived in Olympia in the harbor and drove 40 minutes into the "heart of darkness." After 13 years I moved across that invisible line and moved 5.9 miles outside of civilization to the beach in Eld Inlet. It seemed more or less safe for 17 years.

Who lives outside of civilization?

The vast majority of people who inhabit "The New Appalachia" are multi-generational poor people. They seek anonymity and to be left alone to live their lives as they so choose.

One in three girls and one in four boys will suffer sexual abuse. Growing marijuana and making methamphetamine is endemic and cheap heroin is plentiful. Domestic violence is a common way of life.

The Long arm of the law.

Law enforcement is sporadic on the 326 mile loop circumnavigating the Olympic Peninsula. Some places only have one deputy who works alone and has backup at least an hour away if he or she can make radio contact. The population is well armed. Occasionally a law enforcement official gets shot or stabbed. Sometimes somebody dies. It is a long way to a major hospital when you are bleeding to death.

Meth labs are common and when I lived the village of Moclips a few days a week; I was sternly warned not to randomly leave the main road. I could have been easily killed and made to disappear by the local drug trade.

Poaching is a year round vocation. Children are started young in the fine art of skinning road kill. By age ten most kids can hunt with a rifle. Rabbits, deer, coyote, raccoon, birds and opossum are the usual victims of juvenile gun violence.

Driving and Poaching

Poachers drive the country roads at night with spot lights mounted on their trucks. When they see the glow of an animal's eyes, the full spot light is turned on the animal. Typically, the animal will be temporary frozen and blinded by the light. A pistol, rifle or blast from a shot gun will dispatch the animal. The shooter may be in the truck bed or the cab. It looks less suspicious if the shooters are in the cab and just shoot out the window. The animal is retrieved and thrown in the bed of the truck.

When deer or bear is unfortunate enough to stray into the road; the poaching procedure goes like this. The pickup truck strikes the animal with a greatly reinforced bumper and grill. The driver stops and gets out of the truck with a pistol or rifle. The driver shoots the animal in the brain and throws the animal in the truck bed. The beast is covered with a heavy tarp and the driver drives away. The total time out is less than 60 seconds.

Sometimes a non-hunting car or truck will strike an animal. One of the locals will execute the animal if necessary and dive off with the prize. Hunting seasons and licenses are generally seen as needed by tourists. After all, a local gas station/mom and pop store will make a few buck by selling a license!

When one is in "The New Appalachia," one never asks what kind of meat it is, or from where it came; especially while being a guest. The host will often brag, but it is rude to ask. I avoided this issue mostly because I am a pescaterian. That is a fish eating vegetarian. Although fish poaching is common too.

I once ate a beautiful flakey piece of sturgeon at a restaurant on the coast. The cook came out and said that it was sturgeon and I told him that it was very well prepared. When I asked where he got the sturgeon, he became furtive and mumbled that I must not be from around here! I had accidentally broken the code of behavior! This code applies even in a public restaurant.

An Accidental Adventure

I was driving to Aberdeen from Mud Bay on a Saturday. I decided to take a road parallel to Highway 8. To my chagrin the paved road disappeared and the dirt road was one lane and full of holes.

I couldn't find a place to turn around. I passed several shacks that were inhabited. There were animal skins tacked out on the rails on the porches. I was listening to the radio but it was fading in and out. I could barely hear a county song. My imagination was running wild and I was afraid. I was thinking the song might be that tune from the movie "Deliverance."

I finally decided I'd have to try to turn around because the ruts in the trail were getting deep and muddy. I attempted to turn around in front of a shack that looked unoccupied. I was making short turns on the trail and was beginning to be high centered in the mud. My wheels were spinning and I was losing traction. All of a sudden an old man with Bowie knife leaped from his front porch. I tapped my seven shot 357 magnum which was under my winter coat.

I unzipped the front of my coat about 10 inches and waited to see what was going to happen. He looked at my predicament and smiled. I could see only one front tooth.

He went back into the shack and brought out and ancient looking rope and pulley system. He tied one end of the rope to the front end of my Toyota and the pulleys to a tree, which was about 50 feet away. Then he instructed me to drive while he pulled me all the way around with his pulley system. It worked. He walked up to the passenger side and asked for $10.

I cringed because I didn't have any money on me. I leapt out of the car and opened my trunk. I had a case of cheap beer. If this didn't go well; I was ready to defend my life and the pistol hung heavy under my coat. He laughed and said he would take the beer.

I gave him the beer and he cracked two bottles open. We sat on his porch and looked across the small hillside at a cooling tower which was still standing from the partially built nuclear power plant. The plant will never be finished. The State ran out of money. Like so many things in "The New Appalachia" the money was gone.

I noticed some rabbit skins drying over his stove in his shack and asked about the process for preserving rabbit furs. He was clearly an expert and explained that the procedure is simple and brutal. I marveled at the contrast between nuclear power technology and animal skin preservation.

We shook hands and exchanged names. I drove back to the pavement and drove to the Coast. I have never seen him again. I have not disclosed his name, out of respect for his privacy.

I didn't mind working in the uncivilized world but needed to rest in safety most days. This meant I would drive out at the end of the day. As I grew more smart in the Appalachian like ways; I felt more comfortable leaving normal society. After thirteen years I move just a few miles past mud bay and lived on the Steamboat Island Peninsula at Young Cove on Eld Inlet. There were many educators, social workers, and state workers living out there and I felt safe.

My wife and I raised two sons and the local school was well run. Life seemed almost idyllic. We were paying $400 a month and leasing a spot in a water front mobile home park. Our beach cabin was a double wide module home. At times our income was over $100,000 a year. I had a view of the saltwater beach from my window in my writer's office. I could see: deer, raccoons, river otters, eagles and rarely a whale or two.

The Homeless Arrive

We began to notice a change in our neighbors. They were homeless men and women. They were camping in the woods near our home and they made me nervous. I had worked with homeless people over the last two decades. In my early days, homeless people really seemed to make an effort to live under the radar.

They lived in discreet places and more or less didn't create a scene. They were willing to do day labor and most seemed to be trying to manage traumas gained from childhood or military service. Overall they were just people trying to survive not unlike everybody else.

Nowadays they seem predominately predatory. Within weeks of me noticing homeless people near our home; break-ins all over began to occur. Mail theft became chronic and acute. Things began to disappear.

I had lived peacefully all these years and never worried about my stuff or my safety. In fact, I rarely locked my doors when I lived alone. Later, I took the family to Mexico for a week and accidently left our front window open without a problem. We lived for seven years without locks on our windows and nobody even tried to get in. However, when 25 homeless people began to pillage the area; things changed.

We became even very cautious about stopping at our local (3 miles away) store at night. People were being frightened and cars were being broken into. A couple robberies occurred. It took me 2 years for me to recognize that we were potential targets for crime. Also, there was only one deputy assigned to our end of the county.

It was not just the arrival of the homeless that made living in the wild unsavory. We started to get economic refugees from the city. I have always felt being poor does not automatically mean that you have to live in squalor. The new kind of welfare dwellers seemed to leave: diapers, tampons and rotting food garbage everywhere. This of course attracts rodents and raccoons and other wild animals. In homes I visited, they had field mice crawling all over their counters, floors, and bedding. There are dangerous diseases found in animal feces. One in ten field mice carry Hanta Virus.

This lack of attention to basic health and hygiene, seems to be a symptom of the disintegration of families and individual mental health.

The Lack of Proper Parenting

Many welfare moms and dads seemed to have stopped raising their children. Or maybe they never raised the children. Now, I had to watch for deer and children who would roam our dangerous country roads and night. Even small children would dart in to the roads in the dark. Children do a terrible job of raising themselves. Vandalism started occurring. My shellfish farm on the beach was destroyed. Signs were spray painted with gang symbols. A lady across the road had her solar lights torn up.

One day a heard some kid screaming, "Hurry." I went outside to find 4 kids going through a car load of my belongings which I was taking to the thrift shop in the city. I recognized one child as belonging to a neighbor. I told the group, that it was wrong to steal. The laughed and repeated what I had just said.

I pulled my cell phone out and pretended to call 911. I didn't get cell service in my front yard but that didn't matter.

I went to the house that belonged to the child I recognized. It turned out that all 4 kids were living at the house.

Basically I forced both parents to act like adults for at least a moment. The mom wanted to shirk her responsibility until she realized that this might have dire consequences. The dad just didn't want the police in his house. Who knows what illegal activity was going on. At least he put his foot down for a moment.

The kids were restricted to their yard for a month and never came to my house again.

Time for a Change

So, it wasn't difficult to decide to move to a luxury apartment in gated community in the city. What finally precipitated the move was that my wife said she really wanted a change in our lifestyle. Three days later the land lord agreed to buy our mobile home and we were free. We actually just moved about 8 miles away. We crossed the invisible line back into civilization. The line may be invisible but there is a seriously different culture which is delineated at Mud Bay. I didn't need to worry about safety or the security of our belongings anymore.

I now lived closer to my new neighbors but I rarely hear or see them. However, when I see them, they are happy and friendly. Their children are generally well behaved. A neighbor told me that when a teenager climbed into the giant trash compacter the family was expelled from the community. I guess you must supervise your kids here.

I enjoyed cheap living at the beach before the changes happened. Now we pay $1500 a month. I think you must make $4500 a month to qualify to live here. There is a pool and club house. Somebody else takes care of the maintenance and the landscape.

I have been working in the city now. Everything is close. My banks and several major stores are only 200 yards away. It will take time to grow accustomed to a new way of living. I notice all kinds of little things that are nice. The green areas around the community are more like parks instead of wilderness. Our living space is really almost "hotel clean." I can sit on my second floor sundeck without being menaced by raccoons or big deer or the occasional racing pickup truck. If I want to go to the beach; it is a short drive to my sailboat, in the marina. From there I can visit all of Puget Sound or the San Juan Islands. It turns out that I can still see stars at night from my new front porch, where I have even installed my rain gauge for cocorahs.org. My Weather Station name is Olympia 3.2 SSW.

We still occasionally play tourist and go past Mud Bay. My wife and I are planning road trip the Quinault tribal resort and casino at the beach at Ocean Shores. I am partial to the Squaxin tribal hotel and casino near Shelton. I developed a way to count cards in Black Jack that works.

There are many highly successful tribal operations scattered around the Olympic Peninsula. Much of the region may be called "The New Appalachia" but the shining exceptions to this are the Native American Resorts and Casinos. These tribal businesses reap vast amounts of wealth for the tribes and they really are very important employers for the regions.

The wealth may hasn't drifted to many non-natives yet; but then again the tribal members are willing to work when given a chance.

What keeps the region economically depressed?

Welfare is keeping the region down. Welfare was never meant to be a lifetime career option. Certainly it was never intended as a family trade to be carried on with the next generation. The State of Washington has begun to set lifetime limits on the use of the public dole. But now there seems to be a tremendous number of people on Federal Social Security Disability.

There are many other reasons for the poverty. For example, when people suffer abuse it tends to distract them from work and education. Abuse survivors are more likely to have substance abuse and mental health issues. A meth head makes a poor employee. There are many more factors in this complex issue. I have spent many years working in the wilderness. Maybe somebody smarter than me will figure out how to change the ways of the wild someday. Meanwhile It is time for me to rest.

What was my job?

I had many different roles. For example, I was a private social service provider and a counselor in private practice from 1988 until 2012. I also worked as a teacher and a school counselor. I am a writer at Amazon.com. I presently have written: 73 e-books, 67 paperbacks and 44 audio books.

This has been a most difficult short story to write about. There will be other professionals who will strongly disagree with my perception of "The New Appalachia" or even this informal characterization of the region.

I think they are just ignorant of the facts. My knowledge comes from working and living there. There are high functioning well funded people who live their lives on the Olympia Peninsula. They just stick to their own class and kind. The majority (the poor) are more or less invisible to the well-off. The middle class and wealthy go to their well-paying jobs and socialize at the country club or the tribal resort and casino. The rest of the population generally drinks beer at the sleazy local tavern if they can afford it. They drive home drunk if the police radio playing at the bar indicates that the deputy is far away.

The New Appalachian is fiercely independent of government control except for the monthly welfare checks. For example, about ten years ago the state of Washington State forbid smoking in bars and restaurants. In many bars and restaurants on the coast, it was largely ignored because they generally serve only locals. This once caused me a problem when I stopped at a local eatery late at night. I walked in with a clipboard and everybody thought I was and an inspector for the Department of Health. It was dead silent until I explained to the waitress that I was new in the village and would be stopping in a couple nights a week. Then most people lit up cigarettes or marijuana bongs and went back to their chatting.

On Tuesday and Wednesday nights over a two-year period, I enjoyed sitting by the warm fireplace and eating whatever local seafood was available. I guess at least ½ my meals which were cheap and poached. The company was pleasant and I made many friends. I would then go to my cold cabin on the beach and crawl into a sleeping bag and start the day again at sunrise. Although a was terrified at the possibility of a Tsunami while I slept at night; the rent was very cheap and it saved me a long drive back to civilization.

Epilog

I don't miss living and working in "The New Appalachia." It was hard work and sometimes dangerous. It was rewarding because I am an optimist, and some individuals made successful and happy lives after we spent time together.

My mind returns to a short poem I wrote when I was 18 years old.

We are what we are

We do what we do

We are nothing less

And nothing more than

What we choose to be.

JJ Nugent 1979

Best Regards

James Nugent

11-11-15

Other Books by James Nugent

How I Sailed from Olympia to the San Juan Islands, and Returned Safely

An Alternative Boating Guide to Southern Puget Sound

Twenty Hours under the Sea

Without Speech

Miracles in Young Cove

Home Self-defense

How and Why I lived Aboard

Kayaking Budd Inlet in South Puget Sound

Writing E-books and Making the Perfect Book

I Speak Esperanto

The Rainbow Road and Other Signs of God's Love

Write a Book

Living an Abundant Life, Within Your Means

Social Jujitsu and Powerful Principles for Managing Social Conflict

Advanced Social Jujitsu

Blackjack on My Small Budget

A Little Benedictine Oblate Manuel

Without Speech

All things work

Loving Time with Your Creator

Personal Adventures in a Life of Learning

Loving Time with Your Creator

The Good News about Being Catholic

The Extraordinary Eucharistic Visitor

E-book Writing and Overcoming Barriers to Creativity

Living an Abundant Life Within Your Means

E-book Writing and Organizing Your Ideas

Paddling to the Rhythm of God

My Forty Days for Life 2013

Lifestyle Reality Observing

How to Sail in the Winter

How to Get Your Kid to Move Out

How to Get What Want

Sex, Abstinence, and Happiness

Cynthia Says Radio Show – Anger is a choice

Eight Things You Need to Survive

Three Moms from Hell

Moving and Starting Fresh

More Good News about Being Catholic

The Solo Kayak

Rainy Day Kayak

Night Kayak

Solo Kayak II

Paddles and Water

A Beach Naturalist on Southern Puget Sound

Clean House Clean Life

The Total Catholic Christian

Advanced Social Jujitsu

The Beginning School Counselor

Managing the Most Difficult Students

Not Taking Responsibility

Happiness is a Choice

The Voyages of Saint Bernadett

Living on the Edge of Civilization

Living on the Edge of Civilization

*Available at Amazon.com in Kindle E-Book and or Audible
Book or Paperback*

Living on the Edge of Civilization

Living on the Edge of Civilization

www.ingramcontent.com/pod-product-compliance
Lightning Source LLC
Chambersburg PA
CBHW061952280526
45787CB00004B/1827